In memory of my wonderful husband Mike,

I dedicate this book

to his daughter Elizabeth

and our two grandchildren, Max and Florence

It seems that we are writing less
Does that now mean my fond caress
In print has lost its former glow?
In simple terms the answer's - 'No!'

It's just that we are now a pair
And you with me most times are there …
So I can tell you face to face
Or show you in a close embrace.

I love you so - I don't need rhymes
'Cos you are here at all the times
When poetry flows - I need no verse
To show my feelings short and terse.

Instead in gestures I can show
How much I do adore you so.
The spoken word - once just in print -
I hope gives you a subtle hint.

I only write these stanzas short
To prove I've not forgot to court
Amour courtois is in the past
'Cos now I know new love will last.

Mike

TABLE OF CONTENTS

INTRODUCTION

PRELUDE

INTERRUPTION

AFTERMATH

REVIVAL

Introduction

Are poems the diary of a poet's life, or are they just a diary in verse? A Turn in the Road by Sarah Strange is a brilliant illustration of the former. The 63 poems chronicle the death of her husband, her gradual acceptance of the loss and the eventual triumph of finding love again.

It is an authentic and beautiful portrait of a human being. The diary-like format aids exceptionally well the poetess' description of her husband's brave but silent fight with terminal illness and the pretend-objectivity that the format dictates, the interspersed images of the daily routines of a contented married life convey all the stronger her own anxiety and suffering.

It is striking how the poems are redolent of honesty; the unashamed focus on herself, the depression and loneliness, her finances and jobs, the femininity. Indeed, perhaps the most endearing quality of her verse is their touching femininity; the thoughts of clothes and shopping, the unremitting female insecurity about looks and the conviction that her pain and emptiness will end once a loving mate is found.

Sarah Strange has been writing poems since the age of seven and with her literature-tuned husband they regularly exchanged poems of love. It shows.

Her use of language is rich but also wonderfully accessible and while she expertly varies her rhyme schemes they remain enticingly musical. The colourful but easy complexity of her imaginative connotations is something to behold. Writing, for example, about their last holiday in Barbados, her reference to *"the Trades that many a sail have trimmed"* evokes not just the slave trade and the southern hemisphere trade winds but also the joy of sailing off the Caribbean coast.

Her aphorisms - even the culture-based ones such as *"Carpe Diem"* or *"it's now not then"*, a clever twist to the eternal question of the Hebrew sage of antiquity "if not now, when" – draw instant understanding. They also testify to her English roots. Who wouldn't immediately know what lies behind "Easter Blues".

Sarah Strange's quintessential Englishness is all there; in her proverbs and nursery rhymes, and although the speaking is direct, there is a reticence and an almost stiff upper lip kind of dignity. One must read knowingly to see behind the words the intensity of feelings and even their hidden sexuality. The discreet report on the last months with her husband, *"I slept no longer in your arms"*, is unmistakably a sobbing sigh of need. Similarly, although the description of the re-start of her life is delicately embedded in an analogy of a floating boat

(her body), *"I cried until my body shook with tears…*
a tsunami swamped my mind; I could not speak",
invites a sweetly erotic image of an explosive
enjoining with her new man.

But above all, the outstanding quality of Sarah
Strange's poems is their universality. The human
spirit and emotions that shine through them bring
immediate recognition, association and empathy. It is
an unmissable read for all lovers of verse.

**Stephen NOTI journalist, partisan to art, be it the
stroke of the brush, marble or bronze, sound or
word.**

PRELUDE

Good Grief

"Good Grief!" - an expression often said
With certain flippancy not dread
But who now ponders on this word
Grief's never good – that is absurd.

A period most of us go through
It spans a month or a year or two
Depending whom it is we've lost;
An acquaintance or a former boss

School friend or neighbour down the street
A colleague whom we used to meet
For lunch and chat now and again
A friendship made when on a train.

All these and more fade from our sight
For a while we keep their image bright
Then overwhelmed by daily chores
Our busy lives close memory drawers.

It is only when a date comes round
Or we smell a perfume, hear a sound
That our mind's eye captures them once more
And grief invades us, makes us raw.

The Double Verdict

What I see in you, Mike dearest
Doesn't strike the casual eye
Walking down the street together
There are some who'd wonder why.

Whereas when they look at you, dear,
Summing up is cut and dried.
Of course I'm just your lady love
Why else would they look so snide?

People arc so superficial
They can't see what's crystal clear.
We've got so many things in common;
It would be silly not to share.

Feminine Logic

There's no logic in my mind
That makes him positively defined
As just the man for me;
And yet, absurd as it must sound
He is the only man around
Who lets me be just me.

He has a hand outstretched my way
To tease and tantalize and play.
It's gentle touch shows care;
It tells much of his fear of harm
For I can see upon his palm
That Hope is written there.

Why chase him? Why await his call?
Why do I hesitate withal
To grab this chance for life?
Why, among the million things
I do each day, I think of him
When doubts I have are rife?

The Feeling

No doubt about it - stands to reason
May's the month and spring's the season
No intervention from Above
Is needed when it comes to love.

And yet old Cupid's wily darts
Have pierced the strangest pair of hearts
It can't be true - yet in defence
The feeling balks at all pretence.

Four days will cure this new malaise
But no - it's here and here it stays.
It can't be helped, nor stopped nor cured
It's real, and vibrant - and absurd.

Why - looking through a Looking Glass
Like Alice, shows a pretty pass.
There's not a hope of its succeeding
And yet somehow it sends them reeling.

Life's like that - when you least expect it
The Powers That Be become electric.
And whichever way you cut life's cake
You know there's more than sex at stake.

Presence

May I perch upon your shoulder?
Be a fly upon your wall?
Hide in your tobacco holder?
Just be at your beck and call?

Can I be your silky hanky?
Or the matching tie you wear?
Hanging round you, feeling lanky
Whispering nothings in your ear?

When you write, I'll be the paper -
Please caress me with your pen.
Fold me gently, read me later
I shall be my true self then.

In your meetings you won't see me.
But don't panic or feel hurt.
Above, the light bulb's burning brightly
I'm watching while you do your work.

If colleagues sometimes find you wander
Staring at the vacant air
Let them believe you've time to squander -
Only you need know I'm there!

Not Keeping up Appearances

We're not what you could call a pair -
In shape, or weight or length of hair;
And people have been known to say,
"And which one is your husband, pray?"

But as we've many times remarked
The links exist - they're in the heart.
Appearances are for the birds;
What really counts are not the words.

But why express what we both feel?
That's our secret - it's for real!

INTERRUPTION

Waiting

I sit here waiting for your call
My mobile, switched on, doesn't speak
The house is clean, I've washed the hall.
The sun shines on our troubled week.

I've had some friends pick up the 'phone
But none of them is you, my sweet.
The house seems large when I'm alone
I long to drive you up our street.

Good hands I'm sure are taking care
And soon we'll know what rocks our boat
Meanwhile through window I shall stare
And think of you and me … and hope.

At the Double

The heat brings memories to the fore
Our wedding day in Ninety-Four
And now we reach a double score
A milestone new;
We jog along our merry way
Time passes by, yet here we stay
Enjoying each and every day
Just me and you.

Our house is settled, free from fuss
Sometimes we flick away the dust
But housework doesn't bother us
We do our best
To manage projects, meals and friends
Fit in long, lazy quiet weekends
And on occasion start new trends
Within our nest.

A new stage now lies straight ahead
We hope that bright light will be shed
On why you sometimes stay abed
On sunny days
Should I look into crystal ball?
Perhaps the tarot cards say all?
No, I shall wait for doctor's call
On this new phase.

In and Out

August 3 – the sun beats down
I went out shopping and got brown
The passers-by all smiles – no frown
Summer sees a different town.

Not many neighbours hang around
And local shops have shutters down
A privilege this year I've found
So of your absence there's no sound.

A little check, the doctors said
A minor op, two days in bed
It's best we have a look, they said
A tremor; not yet ten years wed…

This afternoon, I'll bring the car
To pick you up – it isn't far
With luck you won't feel under par
Dare I leave the garage door ajar?

Eternal Barbados

The lapping of the waves
The early morning haze
This erstwhile land of slaves -
Barbados.

This Caribbean isle
With its people who beguile
All with warm and friendly smile -
Barbados.

Luscious growth on every hand
Smooth and sparkling strand
But those tree frogs should be banned!
Barbados.

Floodlit palm trees, velvet sky
A gentle breeze and leaves that sigh
Warm air - humidity is high -
Barbados.

Hibiscus, jasmine, tamarind
Bougainvillea in the wind
The Trades that many a sail have trimmed -
Barbados.

Dining Out in Barbados

He told us that the storm would come
The raindrops followed at a run
The blue sky suddenly went grey
The stars were cloaked in velvet sway.

The noise, the power of the storm
Beat on the roof and drenched the lawn
We heard it, still alive, at dawn
The sky in pieces had been torn.

What of the boats moored off the coast?
They bobbed and dipped like bits of toast
Thrown carelessly upon the waves
Paradise has its share of graves.

The plants bow low, as if in awe
The palm trees curtsy to the shore
We dined with dear friends at "The Tides"
Observing the island's wilder sides.

Cricket at the Tamarind Cove Hotel

The kids play cricket on the lawn
Sunshades are bright, shorts are the norm

From such as these are sportsmen born
The joy of running in the warm,

The sea, deep turquoise blue, is calm
Such peace to troubled souls brings balm.

The Waiting Game

I sit in this grey corridor and wait
What Evil God has brought us to this state?
The personnel glide slowly by
They smile and so we all must try
To keep our inner demons close in check.

Silent Night

This was the last day of your life
The last day I was still your wife
Around me swirled the winter mist
I drove home from our final tryst.

But in our hearts we'd said goodbye
You lay there, eyes closed, almost shy
While all around the nurses came
Ensuring you were not in pain.

The stillness wrapped me like a cloak
Suddenly you seemed remote
A new world, one I could not see
A twilight zone had welcomed thee.

AFTERMATH

Have a Heart

If time had been our ally
We would have made a date,
You were never one to dally
More a river in full spate.

Instead, I find myself alone
In sorrow fit to drown
How I wish you'd ring my 'phone
From somewhere else in town.

The shop displays with garish hearts
Seem pointless, even cruel.
The dominance of red imparts
No passion - I'm love's fool.

Fond Cupid's days with us are past,
He aims at targets new
For us it was too good to last...
Sweet Man - how I miss you.

For a Dear Friend

When last we met in bitter cold
My heart was deep in shock
But winter clouds are tinged with gold
Your kindness helped a lot.

At the funeral you were well wrapped up
But your heart was on your sleeve
When I think of you, my heart warms up
Sweet solace while I grieve.

Sad memories from my mind I cast
On brighter things I dwell
Your birthday has come round so fast
My turn to wish you well!

I know we cannot meet each day
And life can be a trial
But friends like you don't go away
You give me back my smile.

A Glimmer of Hope

February makes one groan
It's cold and short and must atone
For holding us in winter's grip
Where frost and black ice make us slip.

There is not much to recommend
This chill, dark month except its end
Unless of course sweet Valentine
Prompts two hearts to intertwine.

This year harsh winds whip at our coats
We queue at doctors – with sore throats
Bright scarves and hats are on display
As people hurry on their way.

No time to chat – we're in a rush
And can hardly see the roads for slush.
A daily trial – up in the dark
Life just now has lost its spark.

But as I gaze on bare-limbed trees
And frozen lake, the heron sees
Some movement to investigate
While ducks on mirror surface skate.

The owls enjoy this time of year
They hunt in winter moonlight clear
And if you stop and look around
Tendrils peep out from the ground

The city parks, at first sight bare,
In fact remind us – spring is near!

On the March

This month attests time marches on
The skies are blue, the snow has gone
A timid sun comes on the scene
Alighting on new springtime green.

The slightly longer days bring hope
With added warmth – farewell sore throat!
The world wakes up from winter sleep
More neighbours pop out in the street.

The pages of my diary fill
So each day brings its own small thrill
I feel inspired to blonde my hair
Hello friends, I'm here! I'm here!

Easter Sunday

Easter greets us bearing flowers
And those long-awaited showers;
The joyful ring of children's bikes
The absence of a voice – dear Mike's.

The pilgrims all amass in Rome
Where Pope John Paul cannot intone
His Easter blessing – he's too ill
But hangs on with an iron will.

Chocolate, boiled eggs, daffodils
Road works start – I hear the drills!
School is out – the roads clog fast;
This year, so different from the past

Since all our plans have gone awry,
Finds me often wont to cry
But I must put on a brave face
And deck the table out with lace.

Since at my invite come this day
Those who shared our wedding day
Ten years ago in August heat;
Their friendship keeps my memories sweet.

Comings and Goings

The clocks go forward, life moves on
More than three months since Mike has gone
We had high drama in one week
The ailing Pope who could not speak

Has left us and the world awaits
An election in the Papal States
While Monaco grieves at the loss
Of Rainier, Prince and business boss.

As Europe's longest-reigning royal
John Paul and he will make rich soil.
At Windsor all has come to pass
Prince Charles has tied the knot at last.

Camilla's ship seems set at fair
Will Princess Di begin to blur?
The sun brings tourists out, like flowers
Accompanied by April showers.

Some interviews have come my way
The *Grand'Place* sees me every day!
A time of change, new hand of cards
Someone has the trumps and guards -

His hand quite closes against his chest.
I wonder what will happen next?

The Feather

Our wonderful wisteria grows
And sheds its petals on the tiles
May makes me think of cotton clothes;
I ought to look at summer styles.

Meanwhile, your picture's by my side
It emanates a pinkish glow
I peek at it, feel sad inside
I love you, but can't tell you so.

This May 7th's just a date
It has no meaning any more.
Others may still celebrate
But 21 was our full score.

Time travels on - I take the train
Anonymous and second class
I read Dan Brown to ease the pain
Or gaze at fields and watch clouds pass.

A small white feather flutters by
Your message comes through loud and clear
The sun begins my tears to dry
In my heart I feel you near.

Summer Lull

Midsummer's day has passed me by.
Job-wise, I'm still high and dry
Despite the milling crowds in town
I have no work, but do get brown

Because for once the sun is kind;
Hot, humid days mean I don't mind
That I've no guided tour to do.
I can sit, drink beer and think of you.

Had Fate not struck you down in Jan
And I could say I have my man,
Perhaps I would not venture out
And learn what Brussels is about.

You see, I've noticed as I stroll,
The heat begins to take its toll.
Who wants to listen to a guide?
A better bet's to go inside

One of the city's many bars
In a quiet street, bereft of cars.
At last I reach *Place Sainte Catherine*
Just minutes from the tourist scene.

A wooden bench has just come free
So I can pen these thoughts to thee!

On the Sidelines

We know a Belgian summer means
Brief spells of heat, then rain that teems;
Flooded cellars, roofs that leak
And clothes that don't dry for a week!

In 2012 where will I be?
Quietly, sadly, mourning thee
Who so enjoyed spectator sport
The excitement of the tennis court.

Or Rugby, that elusive game
Whose rules I always found arcane.
When "tries" were scored, like lager lout
You shouted, so I just went out.

While you, oblivious to me,
Carried on a running commentary.
The World Cup, such a great event
Left me, to a large extent,

Out on the sidelines so to speak,
Our love "on hold" throughout the week.
But then you would return to me.
Alas, this can no longer be…

A Ring of Roses

The month I've dreaded most of all
Arrives with sunshine in its wake
No one now on whom to call
I must face life without my mate.

We married on a sultry day
Six friends saw our exchange of rings
Ten years ahead seemed far away
But God was up there pulling strings.

How fortunate we had no clue
As we sat down to wedding feast,
Of His secret plans for you:
Now I am both last and least.

The terrace plants thrive in the sun
A new place at your desk I've found
Your pipe smoke made my eyes all run
But now I miss it not around.

Where have you gone? To some strange sphere
Where you can watch my every move?
Give me a sign that you are near
Who else can my poor soul now soothe?

Your company and wise advice,
Your kindness and your loving heart
Were what made life with you so nice.
I don't know why we had to part.

Just Coping

They tell you, you must fill your day
With everything that comes your way.
Go out, ring friends, walk in the street
Discover somewhere new to eat.

So, on this once-so-special date
I brave the raindrops which can't wait
To splash like tear drops down my face.
I try to put my smile in place.

For August, it is rather cool
The town, so busy as a rule,
Seems to my jaded eye to be,
All in slow motion, mocking me.

I arrange to meet a friend for lunch
With barely half an hour to crunch
On crusty French bread, I decide
To forget the day I was a bride.

September Stepping Stone

This month begins in warming sun
Amazing! All my jobs are done
And what is more,
I won't be poor
A Belgian pension soon will come!

Some invoices have now been paid
So certain worries are allayed
The work scene marks,
In fits and starts,
My arrival in a different trade.

My diary still has many gaps
My social whirl is not perhaps
What it once was
But that's because
I'm a single girl again, you chaps!

My neighbours pass the time of day
I spend my life another way
The weeks fly by
Because I try
To put my talents on display.

While others dream of their weekend
I find them very hard to spend
As no one's free
To share with me
A film or dinner with a friend.

September Milestone

Three quarters through September
We're still sweating in the sun
There's lots I must remember
But my guided tours are fun!

Each day remains a challenge
Many bridges must be crossed
It's amazing how I manage
More is gained and less is lost.

Last year's letters bring replies
I've had refunds from the State
Every 'phone call a surprise
An appointment or a date.

So I try to keep myself amused
To compensate my loss
But know, sweet love, if I enthuse
It's just an outward gloss.

A milestone this week I passed
I did a tour in French
My group declared it went too fast
But now I feel less tense.

You gave your all in helping me
I believe you must have known
Your leaving soon would make me free
To soldier on - alone.

Reverie

What will the autumn season bring?
The days are cool, the nights draw in
There's much to play for; where to start?
I hear the beating of my heart.

It reminds me life's not over yet
Bad memories I must forget
But there is much I shall recall
For twenty years we had a ball.

I shall keep my happiness
Of times gone by in treasure chest
Where only I possess the key
And only I can set you free.

Thus in the autumn of my years
I can see you without tears
How blessed I shall surely be,
Remembering all you meant to me.

The Rest is Silence

Without fixed hours, it's quite a task
To fill my days; what's past is past.
Perhaps you left so I would find
A way of living less unkind.

I know you suffered quite a while
In pain that tried to cramp your style.
You knew you'd drawn a rotten card
And that is why you tried so hard –

The day of reckoning to ignore
But your expression said it all.
I admired you for the way you fought
A courageous lesson you have taught.

Because you would not share with me
This hidden death, your destiny,
I remained for months quite unaware,
How little time we still could share.

Then the shades all gathered round
And your loving voice made no more sound
You slipped away without a cry
Sweetheart, we never said goodbye...

A Sign of the Times

The calendar upon the wall
Announces Scorpio once more,
But what is that to me this time,
Save the subject of another rhyme?

We used to joke the stars were wrong
Sagittarius fails to get along
With watery Scorpio who runs deep;
In jealous arms she will not sleep.

We concluded, if you get my drift,
This theory needed but short shrift
Since we were happy from Day One
Irrespective of our moons and sun!

Now autumn with its russet hues,
Warm sunshine and enchanting views,
Reminds me that this time last year,
The Indian summer of your career,

We flew to Prague on happy flight
Our family group dined out at night.
On Charles' Bridge you posed for me;
You smiled and so I could not see

Beneath that stylish hat you wore,
The suffering I now know you bore.
Prague's fabled castle all aglow
Was in the background, this I know.

I took the photo out again;
With hindsight it is very plain
With all your heart and very soul
You were acting out your finest role.

Emptiness

It's ten months since you had to leave,
Ten months now I've had to grieve
In troubled dreams I see your face.
But awaking there's an empty space.

Are you watching over me?
How I wish that you could be
Beside me as I struggle on
It sure is lonely with you gone.

I want to tell you all my news
And share, as in the past, our views
On life, on people, world events
So much, alone, does not make sense.

I'm told that Time will help me bear
The realisation you're not here
This gaping hole I cannot fill
Perhaps, indeed, I never will.

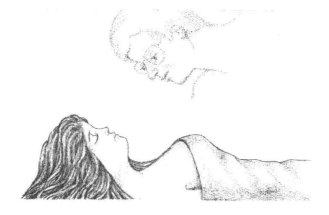

A Whole New Meaning

Most Novembers we have known
Have been spent travelling far from home.
The first as holiday we'd get
So months ahead we oft would set

Aside this "long weekend" and drive
To England, glad to be alive.
Why, only last year on this day
Prague's beauty held us in its sway.

Today I realise something new
A prompting, does it come from you?
To contemplate our love cut short
I pray for strength but feel distraught.

I follow others down the street
And end up at your last retreat
A mass of flowers on every side
I placed your rose, and yes, I cried.

How comforting this day can be
Thousands come here just like me
To share a moment, quiet and still;
We love you, and we always will.

Grey Thoughts

This time last year we met in town
I dressed your "Rita"* in her gown,
In the wings you watched the play
Quiet, I thought, and rather grey.

We joked and wished our actors well
Then struck the set, but who could tell
This was to be your final play
It seems like only yesterday.

Then came my birthday; you weren't well
More tired than usual, I could tell.
To see the Doc you took the bus
Discreet as always without fuss.

Yet still I did not see the signs
Or read too deeply between lines.
Your tiredness I had come to know
The fact you walked upstairs so slow.

 I slept no longer in your arms
Something rankled, gave me qualms.
I realise now, a year ahead
Your life by then hung by a thread.

The last few grains of golden sand
Through the hourglass were panned
Each so small and barely seen
But together they would break our dream.

*"Educating Rita" by Willy Rushton

Looking Beyond

No poem on my breakfast plate,
It's true we cannot now relate
Our feelings on another year
The chain is broken, that is clear.

So I am left to muse awhile
And create perhaps another style
But monologues are not for me
Perhaps I can your medium be?

I feel you prompting me to go
And make new contacts, here below
I do your bidding, but my heart
Is frozen, it has lost its spark.

The future seems uncertain now
But winter fields still need the plough
We can't make Father Time stand still
Perhaps tomorrow brings a thrill.

I still feel so attached to thee
Just like a branch does to a tree
Last year the frost attacked the root
But in the spring new leaves will shoot!

First Anniversary

On 4th Jan I ate chocolate cake,
It was a sweet reminder;
A softer start this year I make
I feel that Fate is kinder.

What matters is the here and now
You gave me strength to follow.
I shall survive I know, somehow
There's light in my tomorrow.

Your wedding band, a perfect ring
Surrounding me with love
Is in itself a holy thing
Empowered from Above.

An outward sign, a sense of peace
A full year's run its course
Our special bond will never cease
It gives me inner force.

I carry you within my heart
At times I hear your voice
Prompting my new life to start,
I'll act upon my choice.

Thus as I find myself in charge
New decisions will be made
I promise faithfully to discharge
My actions, unafraid.

Why take on fear? It bodes but ill
You taught me to let go
Life still has the power to thrill
I feel it must be so.

The Gold Pen

My second Easter without my Love,
A certain stillness in the air,
I miss him calling me his dove
What would he think of my long hair?

Would he be proud of how I cope,
Without his guiding hand nearby?
Our life together seems remote
Memories flutter and go by.

And then about my daily round
His gold pen in my hand I see
He searched but it could not be found
Those last few months he spent with me.

It stressed him out and caused him *angst*
But worry chased it from his mind
Then Suffering and Death closed ranks
So only later did I find

It nestling in a favourite suit
Grown too small for swollen frame
Glistening like a polished fruit
Beckoning for me to claim.

I look upon it now and then
Remembering how he penned his rhymes
A gift from God from way back when,
And recall our lost but happy times.

Daffodils at Easter

Thoughts of you oft cross my mind
A bit like Wordsworth's daffodils
Plagiarism of a kind
In middle age the theme still thrills.

This metaphor, where can it go?
You are not yellow, it's not spring
And yet your image seems to flow
Like the lake, a moving thing.

I have no couch on which to lie
My mind goes vacant when I'm tired
But it's true I see you in mind's eye
Something stirs, my muse is fired.

Wordsworth's ode I learned by heart
I recited it for my exam
Since then it's always been a part
Of me, the way I really am.

Proust with his dratted *madeleine*
Roamed at leisure in the past
Some memories remain the same
Burnt on your soul, they are stuck fast.

One Easter, it was long ago
You took me to the Yorkshire dales
We walked and you were proud to show
The daffs that had survived the gales.

So as in solitude I lie
Reflecting on what might have been
I see you with your head held high
Walking past that Lakeland stream.

Sunny Thoughts

Suddenly the fog is lifting,
By that I mean I see the sun
Farewell all that paper sifting
What a long way I have come.

Bleak January a year ago
Nothing in my life made sense
Mike had left me here below
Frustrated, lonely and intense.

No point seeking what is lost
There's no future in the past
I must move on, not count the cost
In a new role I've been cast.

Reflecting on this dreary time
Where scarce a beam of light broke through,
I now can pen a brighter rhyme
And plan more carefully what to do.

It's hard with no one by my side
And the learning curve is steep,
But success is coming as a guide
And I know I have enough to eat.

On the Springboard

Decisions now come thick and fast
Happiness is mine at last
It's time to cast off what is past
And move ahead,
The weather seems to fit my mood
Despite the rain I do not brood
Saddened thoughts cannot intrude,
I find instead -

Courage is coming back to me
In some strange way I now am free
To become the one I want to be
With no holes barred.
A world trip to my distant kin
Who stand beside me thick and thin
And understand the state I'm in,
Makes life less hard.

There will be days when I am down
Behind a mask of happy clown
But I must banish scowl and frown
On guided tour.
Who knows what the future brings?
I hope more roundabouts than swings
In any case a host of things
Now to explore!

Unspoken Thoughts

A gorgeous late autumnal day,
Blustery winds keep frost at bay
My lost love, this is your birthday
Or would have been
It is, however, not to be
For from this life you are set free
I live now with your memory
Still fresh and green.

The news of global warming speaks
Belgium enjoys late summer peaks
We've had so little rain for weeks
And all is dry
I wonder, but I never asked,
Whether at your daily task
You realised this would happen fast
Did you know why?

So as I now enjoy the views
Of autumn leaves in myriad hues
Which help me chase away the blues
Deep down inside
It occurs to me to think out loud
That you, who loved a theatre crowd,
Had always known it was allowed
The Truth to hide…

Love is Love and not Fade Away

"The Stones" old song came back today,
"Love is love and not fade away";
Dear Mike, your face and voice grow faint
My heart, still lonely, makes complaint.

Down the tunnel, far away
My mind's eye sees you every day
With gentle smile but words too soft
Like a little bird you fly aloft.

The more I try to grasp your hand
The more I now can understand
Our life must move in different spheres
Where you are gone, there are no tears.

I can't yet move to pastures new
Because my thoughts still turn to you.
We shared so much for two decades,
How come your face before me fades?

The Afterglow

Christmas looms but still no snow
And everyone is on the go
With cards and letters on the mat
Life and all its joys come back!

The emails flood in, some surprises
Friends and invites and mince pies-es
Deep in the cellar I unearthed
My decorations for Christ's birth.

The winter solstice, shortest day
Pine cones, mistletoe on display
For pagan rite or Christian feast
Incoming mail has much increased.

I reflect upon another year
Wishing still my man was near
Yet life goes on, I have no choice
So I listen to my inner voice.

A crowded diary, many friends
Films, events, outings, trends
Dear Mike's estate is now complete
I can plan those whom I want to treat.

Determined not to mope and pine
Though that is how I feel sometime
I keep Mike's candle burning bright
And see my future bathed in light.

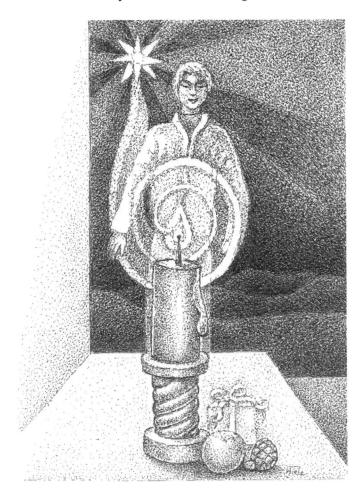

Apprehension

Lost in a sea of waves
Buffeted by this life's storms
Longing for a word that saves
A friendly hug, a word that warms.

Outside are people on their way
Do they seek this pool of calm?
There's something out there, who can say
When it will come, this soothing balm?

It's true perhaps, we drift away
Losing sight of God's warm light
We move on slowly and betray
Our fears - and yet we hold on tight.

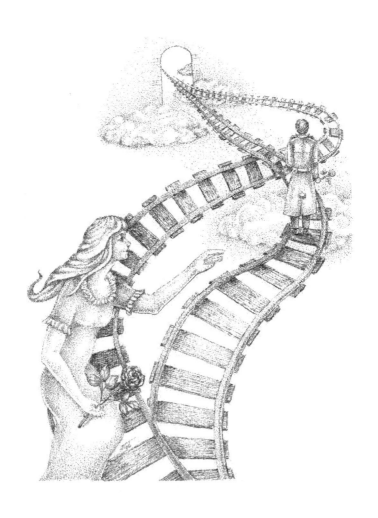

The Man Across the Street

It seemed to me as I left the bank
I saw a well-loved silhouette
The wavy hair a trifle damp
For it had rained and all was wet.

It was just a glimpse, a fleeting glance
Of a man in beige I thought I knew
But it set my heart all of a dance
I sort of hoped it might be you.

My brain soon told my heart, "Be still.
What you desire cannot be true".
All the same I felt a little thrill
And remembered how we once were two.

Fate plays tricks now you have left
My life runs on a single track
Of its engine driver quite bereft
Full steam ahead – no turning back.

In a Café

A mild day – the sun breaks through
It's Thursday – what am I to do?
My emails went out at New Year
To all my friends both near and dear
But few are those who pen replies
I live in hopes of a surprise.
The sales have started; shoppers go
Where the bargains are on show
But have I really need of these –
Remaindered, wilting Christmas trees?

A lucky few are still away
On sandy shore or palm-fringed bay.
But I, who with my thoughts sit here
In a local café, without cheer
Observe the other lonely souls
Who drift in from the winter cold.
Two men drink beer and seem engaged
In discussing business or their trade.
A man plays on the slot machine
A couple, silent, sit and dream.

It could be the Beatles' "Penny Lane"
And Eleanor Rigby is my name;
A chink of coins, the jackpot's won
The winner, unmoved, takes just one
From the pile of Euro cents
And tries his luck again, intense.
I marvel at this village scene
Radio crackling, floors unclean
And constant swinging of the door;
And wonder - surely life is more?

Friday Blues

I'd like to think my days I fill
With every evening a big thrill
I don't feel over that damned hill
At least, not yet.
But still, despite my many friends
And all those emails each one sends
I'm left on Fridays with loose ends
And empty net.

There must be others in my shoes
Not everybody wants to booze
But where to go to and enthuse
With other souls?
It's lonely wandering in the park
A film? Just sitting in the dark
It seems to me the choice is stark
I need new goals.

A feeling prompts me deep within
As memories of my man grow dim
He would not want me to give in
It's now not then!
High summer, so I'll wear bright clothes
And sport new sandals, paint my toes
And smile until the feeling goes

Carpe Diem!

A Blue Tuesday

It's Tuesday, end of March and cold
No letters for me - I'm alone
Incoming emails have been sparse
Beside me lies my silent phone.

I ask myself: what can I do?
Are all my efforts quite in vain?
Not one reply has come my way
I admit to finding life a strain.

Today, by way of change I cleaned
Kitchen and dusty entrance hall
I threw my grubby jumpers in
Washing machine on lower floor.

It's Easter soon; the shops are filled
With tempting chocolate eggs, gift-wrapped
School's out, the exodus begins
Families eager, cases packed.

The grey skies seem to threaten rain
But I cannot stay inside all day
I feel I have to get some air
Let's chase those cobwebs clean away!

Where is the Key?

There must be others in my boat
Trying to keep their thoughts afloat
When spring returns and buds burst forth
And the wind veers East instead of North -

Who feel that life, though good, could be
Much nicer spent again as "we".
God knows I'm not a stay-at-home
But crowds just make me more alone.

I've joined new groups and spread my net
But all the fishes that I get
Though fun - are female, or in pairs,
Or gay men wrapped in long affairs.

Somewhere must be a lonely man
Who muddles on as best he can
Trying to make sense of Fate
As death has robbed him of his mate.

I wonder if these souls will meet;
Joys when shared are twice as sweet
Someone Up There has the key
The thing is - will it fall to me?

A Sad Plea

I am thinking it is August
Almost my wedding day
The memories grow dim with time
The slate wiped clean away.

At sixty, what can one expect?
I still feel young at heart
There must be someone fun somewhere
But hell, where should I start?

I've tried to look my best when out
Perhaps I've over sold?
The one or two men whom I've met
Were nice, but oh, so old!

OK, so friends help pass the time
Be they single or in pairs
But I'd like a special friend for me
Life blossoms when one shares.

Must I grow old without a mate?
Why are men so scarce?
What must I do to change my fate
Apart from writing verse?

In Memoriam

The Bible says three score and ten
Is the allotted span of men
But you'd have chalked up seventy-two
If cancer had not taken you.
Had you but lived upon this day
Instead of passing on, my way -

Would still be bound in happy state
And we'd be out to celebrate.
Instead I make believe you're here
And fleetingly can feel you near.
We all remember your warm heart
The sunshine you would oft impart -

To friends and colleagues, theatre crowd
Who miss you still; so I am proud
To here recall, on this, your day
The spark you kindled back in May
In eighty-three when our paths crossed
That's why, alone, I feel so lost.

Easter Blues

A blazing sun in cloud-free sky
It's Easter Day; I wonder why
Despite the milling crowds around
I still feel much more lost than found.

Alone and lonely aren't the same
But on this day I dare complain
Where are my friends? Not all have fled
There must be some at home instead

Tending gardens, weeding plants
Planning holidays in France
Filing papers, cleaning stoves
Or kneading dough and making loaves.

Perhaps they're out in leafy lanes?
It seems that everyone has claims
Upon their time as no one's free
To spend a little time with me...

Heartfelt

Another wedding day goes by
I cope, reflect but do not cry
Inside my head my tears still flow
This is a secret none must know.

I focus all my thoughts these days
Discretely and in quiet ways
On those who like myself have lost
A loved one and still count the cost.

Those yet untouched, it seems to me,
Repeat with ease *"mais c'est la vie"*
But we who through this torment pass
Have nerves as brittle as cut glass.

The wound is deep and goes in far
But to the world we hide the scar
It's a miracle our heart stays strong
As somehow we still muddle on.

Now each year as this date comes round
I no longer feel so honour bound
And anguished that we had to part
For I have known a loving heart.

The Poem by my Plate

The day dawns – sun dispels the frost
Nearly all November days are crossed
I gaze into the pale blue sky
And imagine happy times gone by.

Today, the 29th appears
I'm sixty-two. Who really cares?
I think of Mike, my life's soul mate
And his poem by my breakfast plate…

Alas, although my friends recall
My brand new year, it's not at all
The same when you are on your own
Beside a silent telephone.

Though oft on business trip abroad
He always managed to record
In witty couplets every time
His feelings couched in clever rhyme.

I know that I should not complain
Or dwell upon this sad refrain
But every year I find it hard
To accept the passing of my Bard!

93

A Sense of Loss

I'm a ship without a sail,
I'm Jonah without his whale,
I'm a spade without a pail
I'm alone
I'm a pen devoid of ink
I'm a bar run out of drink
I'm a film star with no mink
I'm alone.

I'm a needle lacking thread
I'm a baker out of bread
I'm a pencil without lead
I'm alone
I'm a tree devoid of leaves
I'm a hive without its bees
I'm a cold that cannot sneeze
I'm alone.

I am footsteps without feet
I'm a bird that cannot tweet
I'm one drumstick not a beat
I'm alone
What's a sky devoid of stars?
A band without guitars?
Flowers without a vase?
But life alone?

Life on Hold

I'm in a funny frame of mind
Though the August sunshine has been kind
My calls to friends have been ill-timed
They're not at home
The tourists certainly have come
But in this heat a walk's no fun
Lured to cafés - every one
So I'm alone.

I'm trying hard to fill my days
But it seems whichever way I gaze
I'm firmly stuck in waiting phase
Business is slack
Via Internet my message flow
Has plummeted to very slow
Today not even one "hello"
I've lost the knack!

On All Saints' Day

All Saints' Day - stark and cold and wet
Hiatus but we can't forget
Those we have most loved and lost
Life's treasures we have come across.

Each one leaves footprints in our soul
Whether long trek or single stroll
Their images forever sweet
Conjure memories incomplete.

Try as we may the visions fade
Though details linger slightly frayed
A turn of phrase, a laugh, a smile
A moment that was shared awhile.

The heart and logic whirl apart
My deep red rose ignites a spark
As somehow I am caught in time
And catch a glimpse of the divine.

Equanimity

November the Sixteenth looms again
Though you are on a higher plane
I reflect on how old you would be
If you were still on earth with me.

I've worked it out - you're seventy-five,
White-haired, distinguished, warm, alive
Continuing your stage career
How perfect you would be as "Lear"!

Of Max and Florence you'd be proud
Like you they stand out in a crowd
And overflow with *joie de vivre*
For a moment I forget to grieve…

A Meditation

It's as if the light has been snuffed out;
All of a sudden in comes doubt
Certainties of your life together
Happiness on the "Never Never"
That sunshine that you took for granted
That loving seedling carefully planted
Those hopes and dreams that you both shared
When you told each other how you cared
Have somehow slipped right from your grasp
So there's no future – only past.

The dark clouds gather; friends are kind
But turmoil takes hold of your mind
How can they know what you feel?
Bereavement knocks you off your keel.
Whether sudden or a long time coming
A loved one's death is harsh and numbing.
At first you don't know where to turn
As memories catch you, feelings churn
A chance remark can bring you down
Life has lost its spark, you drown.

Then one day (I've been there, I know),
Those stagnant waters start to flow
Pale sunlight through that darkness streams
And although sad, you make new dreams
It's a different life, not what you chose
But time offers all of us a rose.
With windows open, a light breeze
Causes a rustling of the leaves
As the spirit flows into your heart
And you find the courage to re-start.

REVIVAL

Red and Blue

Just another day with no fixed aim;
This "floating" feeling is a strain
When will life speed up again?

No phone calls, emails, passers-by
It's as if the well has been drained dry
Thwarted in everything I try.

At least the terrace plants enthuse
In a riot of deep mauves and blues
Do they reflect my inner views?

In other years I plumped for red
Geraniums - each with scarlet head
Like poppies, reminders of the dead.

But blue provides a peaceful mask
So pinning this colour to my mast
Perhaps I've turned the page at last.

Unexpected

A chance encounter months ago,
Emails exchanged; how can one know
What lies ahead? Not me, that's sure
Over a coffee, let's explore!

A dinner date, good Thai cuisine
An exchange of frank views in between
Another coffee, lots more chat
Knowledge gained on this and that.

A long walk in the beech tree wood
The conversation flowed, was good.
It's odd; I feel I know this guy
Yet we've just met – I wonder why.

No crossroads reached, no boats are burnt
No one can judge the wind, I've learnt.
For now let's say the boat sets sail
The painter detached from its nail!

Starting Over

It's just another day for some
A cloudy sky, no trace of sun
And I don't want to jump the gun
But something's new;
There's a certain lifting of my mood
I let my feelings now intrude
Into my thoughts and must conclude
The sun streams through.

Someone's stepped across my path
A little flame burns in the hearth
And what's more, he makes me laugh
Life is so short;
For a decade I've been on my own
I've friends of course who sometimes phone
A few have been my stepping stone
When life was fraught.

But all you out there know the score
Superficial contacts are a bore
You're often left there wanting more
Than they provide;
So it's wonderful to find a man
Who's also lonely and who can
Be caring – not an "also ran" -
To stand beside …

Watery Thoughts

I cried until my body shook with tears
It's something that I haven't done for years
A warm and heartfelt sadness wet my cheek
A tsunami swamped my mind; I could not
speak.

I thought about the pond in which I lie
Sheltered from the river flowing by
And my boat with both its oars attached with
hope
And felt a gentle breeze come down the slope.

There are pebbles washed with ripples by my
feet
My shoes now lie discarded paired up neat
Small wispy clouds no longer block the sun
And shadows all around are on the run.

Should I take the boat and leave the fateful
shore
Say farewell to the past and now explore
The treasures which lie hidden in the stream
Or sit upon my rock alone – and dream?

Setting Sail

Every day brings fresh surprises
Amazing joys in time of crisis
Wide avenues come into view
With prospects challenging and new.

Routine is dull, yet reassuring
But in a lull, life can be boring.
So Fate is ruthless when it strikes
And once-safe certainties ignites.

Deep in the ashes, fertile soil
Where tiny green shoots now uncoil
And reach towards the springtime air
A brand new pattern soon forms there.

The chips are down, the die is cast
The race is on, the pace is fast
Caught up whether we will or no
Breathless, cresting on the flow.

The brake released, the gear engaged
Ahead a feast too long delayed
In a whirlwind swept up, my arms flail
The captain and the ship set sail!

Index of first lines

Printed in Great Britain
by Amazon